So You Want To Be An Artist!

Learn to Draw

Activity Book

Bobo's Children Activity Books

BOBO's
CHILDREN ACTIVITY BOOKS
COLORING, DRAWING & ACTIVITY BOOKS FOR CHILDREN

Copyright 2016

INSTRUCTIONS FOR DRAWING:

THIS HOW-TO DRAWING BOOK CONSISTS OF IMAGES THAT ARE PLACED ON GRIDS. THERE IS AN EMPTY DRAWING BOX WITH GRIDS THAT WILL SERVE AS YOUR PRACTICE SPACE. TO COPY EACH IMAGE, DRAW PARTS OF THE IMAGE PER GRID AND PUT THEM ON THE BLANK GRIDS. SOUNDS DIFFICULT? NOT REALLY. TRY IT FIRST!

IT'S OKAY IF YOU DON'T COPY THE IMAGE PERFECTLY. AFTER ALL, DRAWING IS ABOUT THE EXPRESSION OF YOUR PERCEPTION AS WELL AS YOUR HAND STRENGTH AND CONTROL.

WHEN YOU'VE COPIED THE IMAGE, GO AHEAD AND COLOR IT NEXT! WE'RE EXCITED TO SEE WHAT YOU CAN DO!

DRAW
THE
IMAGE

DRAW
THE
IMAGE

DRAW
THE
IMAGE

DRAW
THE
IMAGE

DRAW
THE
IMAGE

DRAW
THE
IMAGE

DRAW
THE
IMAGE

DRAW
THE
IMAGE

DRAW
THE
IMAGE

DRAW
THE
IMAGE

DRAW
THE
IMAGE

DRAW
THE
IMAGE

DRAW
THE
IMAGE

DRAW
THE
IMAGE

DRAW
THE
IMAGE

DRAW
THE
IMAGE

DRAW
THE
IMAGE

DRAW
THE
IMAGE

DRAW
THE
IMAGE

DRAW
THE
IMAGE

DRAW
THE
IMAGE

DRAW
THE
IMAGE

DRAW
THE
IMAGE

DRAW
THE
IMAGE

DRAW
THE
IMAGE

DRAW
THE
IMAGE

DRAW
THE
IMAGE

DRAW
THE
IMAGE

DRAW
THE
IMAGE

DRAW
THE
IMAGE

DRAW
THE
IMAGE

DRAW
THE
IMAGE

DRAW
THE
IMAGE

DRAW
THE
IMAGE

DRAW
THE
IMAGE

DRAW
THE
IMAGE

www.ingramcontent.com/pod-product-compliance
Lightning Source LLC
Chambersburg PA
CBHW080535030426

42337CB00023B/4739